MW01152085

What Are Germs and Why Do They Make You Sick?

A Children's Disease Book
(Learning About Diseases)

BABY PROFESSOR
EDUCATION KIDS

Speedy Publishing LLC
40 E. Main St. #1156
Newark, DE 19711
www.speedypublishing.com

Copyright 2016

All Rights reserved. No part of this book may be reproduced or used in any way or form or by any means whether electronic or mechanical, this means that you cannot record or photocopy any material ideas or tips that are provided in this book

Oh, my! Germs are around us. They are there, beside you, in front of you, and everywhere. But we can't see them. They are either good or bad. Although not all are harmful, we still have to be very, very careful.

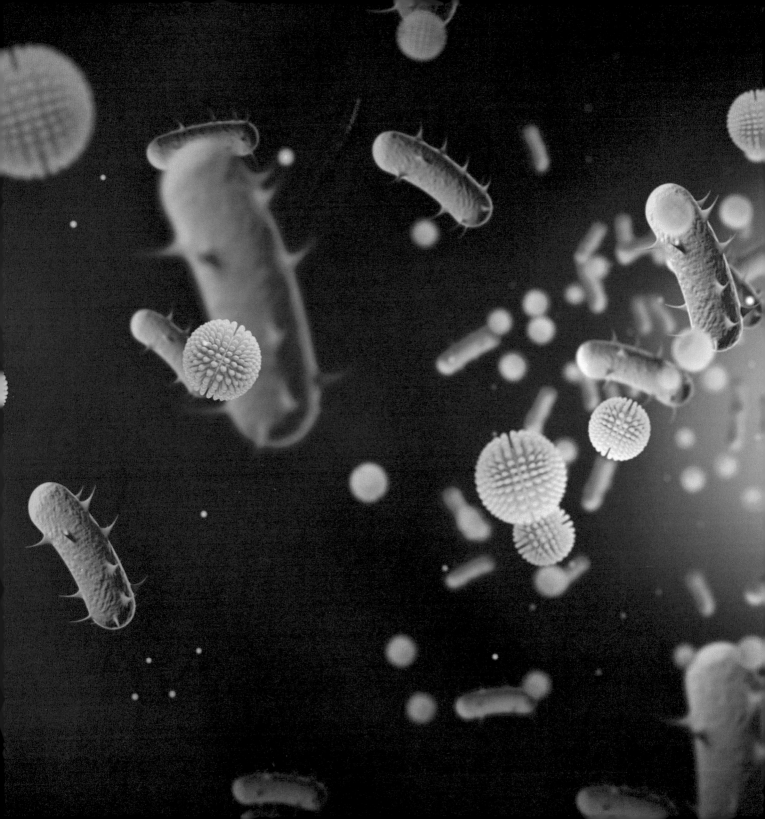

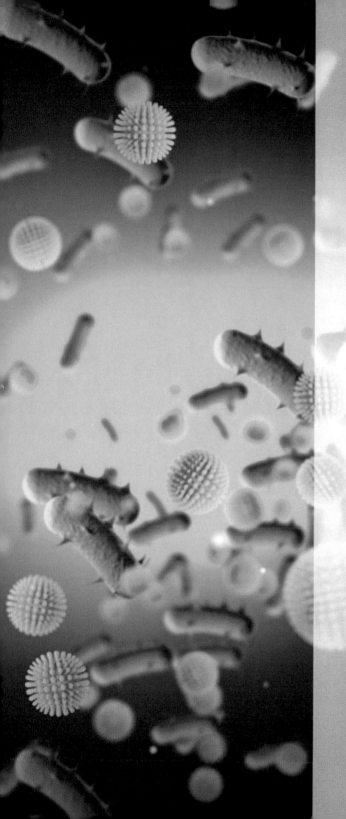

In this book you learn important information about germs. Read on and find out why germs make us sick. Are you ready to fight the germs?

Germs are everywhere. They are present in all kinds of places. Some of them make us sick. With this fact, we get to know how amazing our body is. Our body is a most fantastic machine. It works very hard to keep us alive. It pumps blood, it lets us move and think, it digests our food and it protects us from harmful germs. Our body really works hard to fight germs off and to keep us healthy.

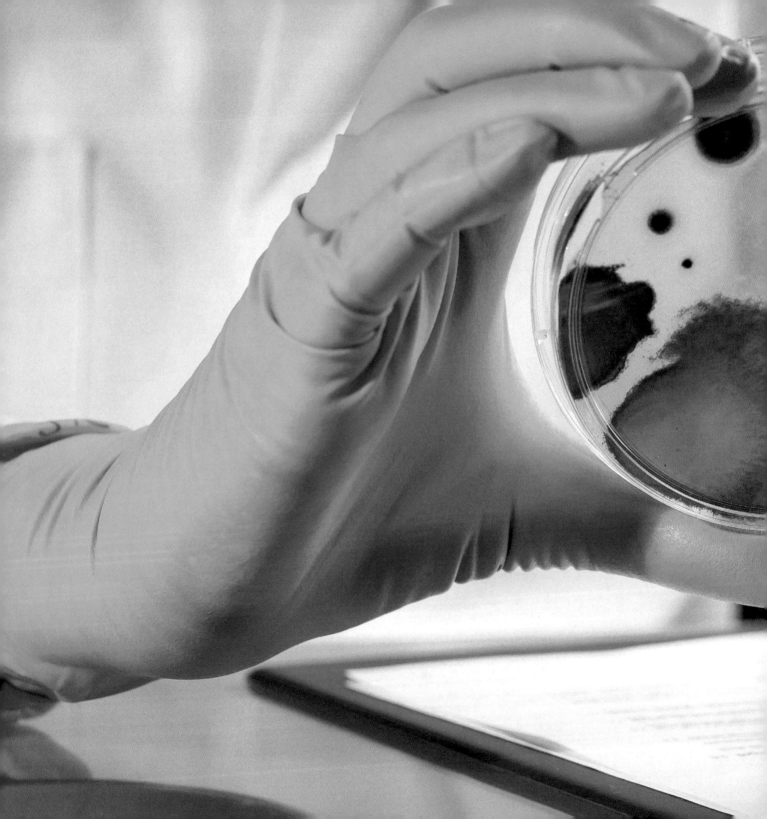

What are germs? These are very tiny invaders that can make us sick. They are microscopic which means we can't see these nasty creatures with our naked eye. Germs are also known as pathogens.

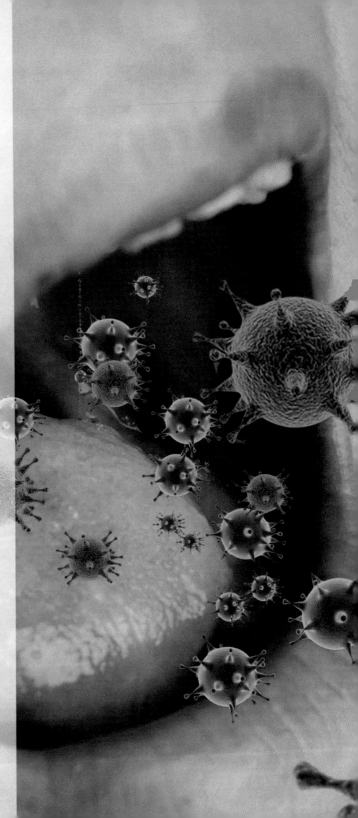

Germs are tiny organisms. Even though they are that tiny, they can cause diseases. They are tiny but they are somehow terrible. They are sneaky. We should be aware that germs can get into our body unnoticed! We just feel their presence once we are already sick.

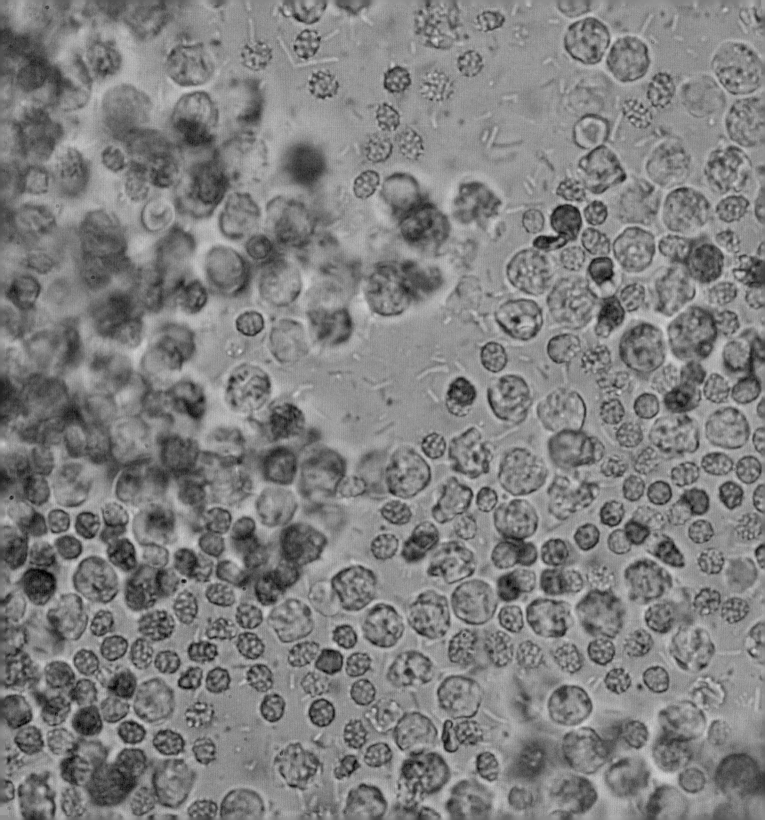

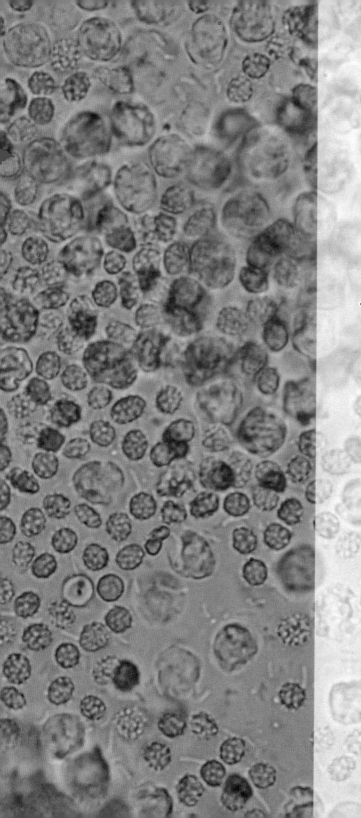

Here are the main types of germs, the tiny and terrible invaders. Some of them can make us terribly sick. Let's get to know each one of them.

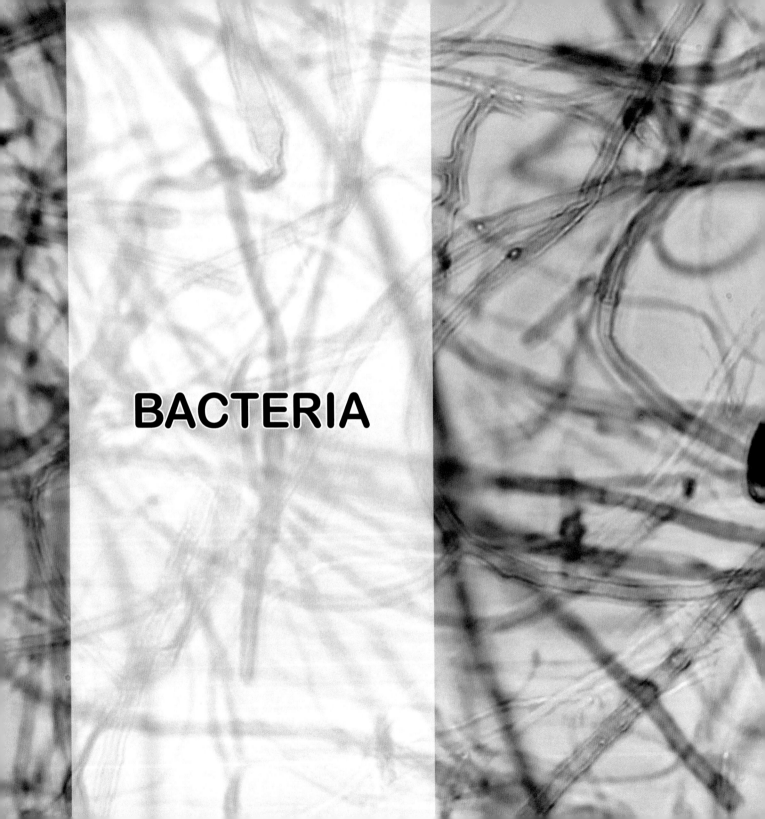

BACTERIA

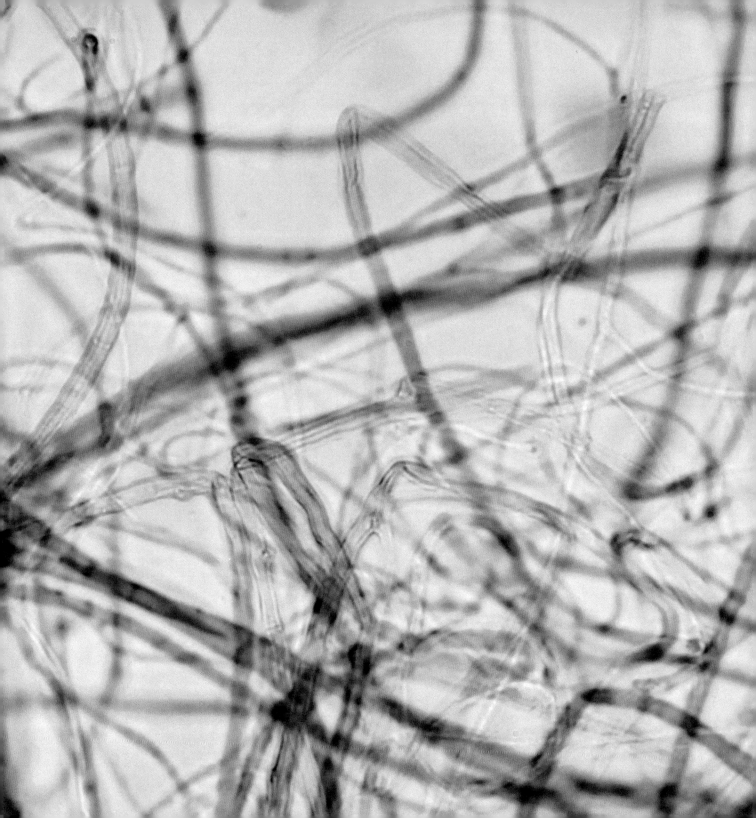

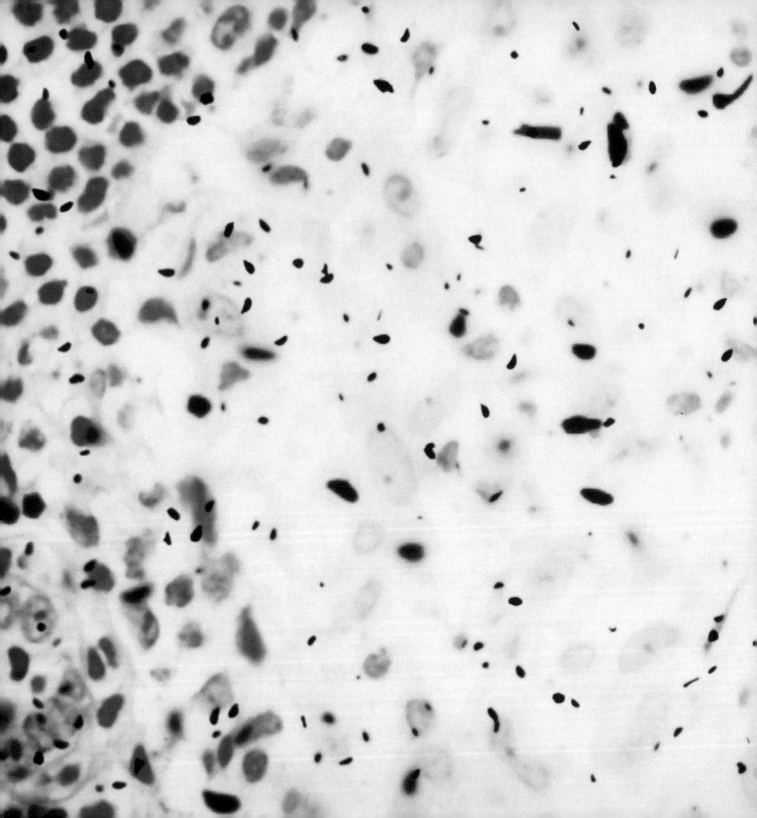

They are one-celled invaders. Their environment is their source of nutrients for them to live and multiply. One of their environments is our body. It could be you. When they get into our system they can cause infections. These include sore throats, pneumonia, and ear infections. However, not all bacteria are bad. Some of them are good and help our body function well. The bacteria that live in our intestines are considered good. They keep the body's systems in balance and help our digestive system. They are the helper germs. Scientists use good bacteria to make vaccines.

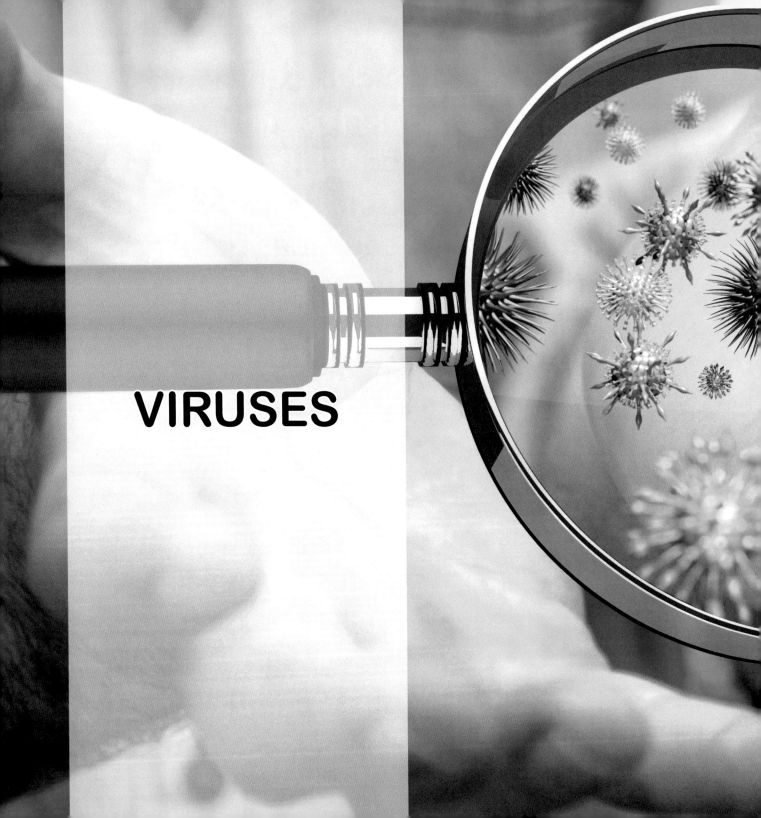

VIRUSES

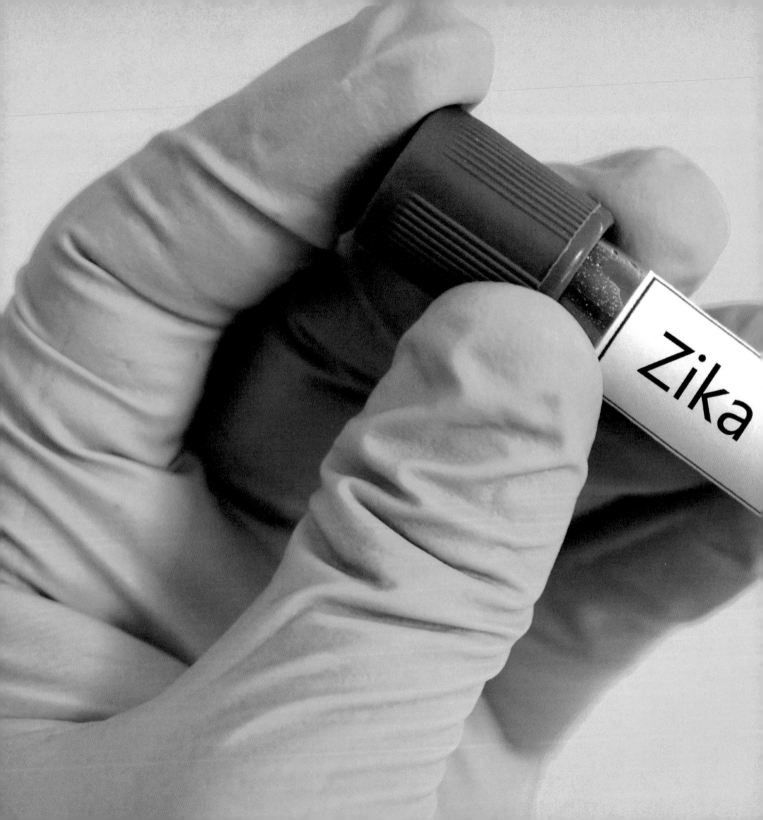

Viruses can definitely make us sick. They cause many diseases, such as flu and measles. Viruses need to live inside the living cells in order to grow and live. They can't survive long when they are outside their hosts. That is why viruses are found in plants, animals, and humans. They spread easily once they get into our bodies. They can't survive if they have no host. The host is where the virus lives.

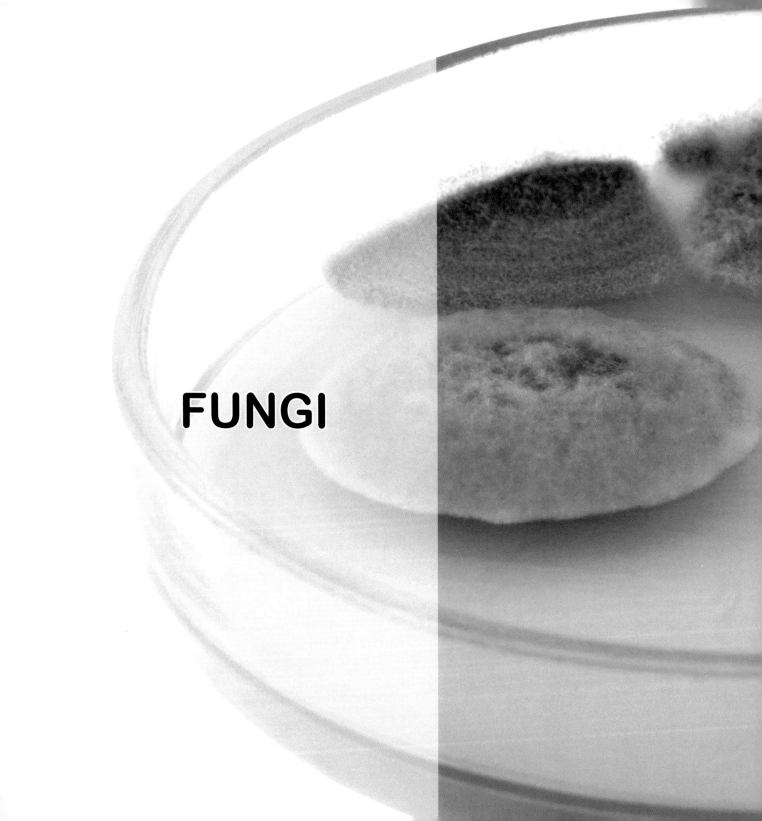

FUNGI

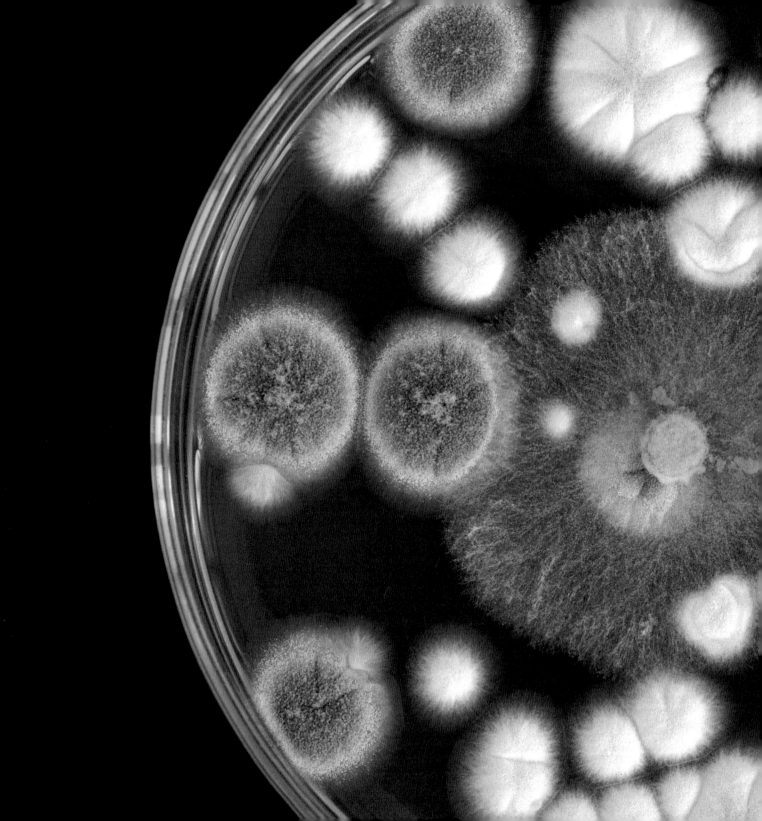

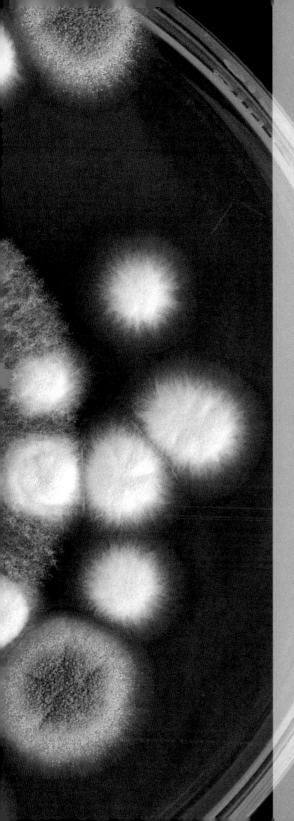

These creatures are made up of many cells. These are multi-celled invaders. They appear like plants. Hence, they are described as plant-like organisms. These creatures get their food from plants, animals, and people. The damp and warm places are their favorite habitats. If one has athlete's foot, that itchy thing between toes, we can say that the person has fungi on him.

PROTOZOA

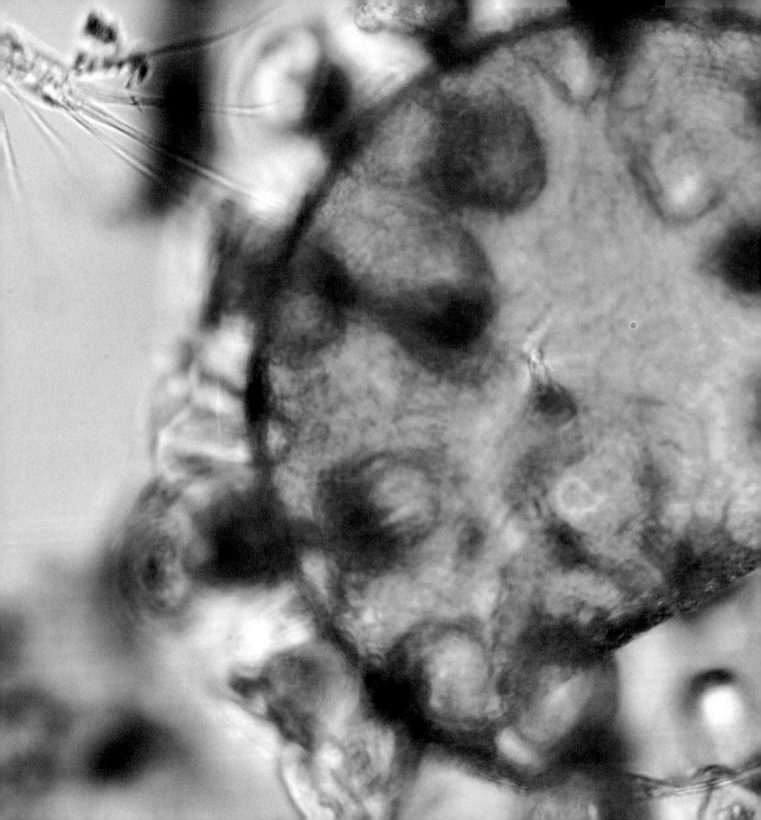

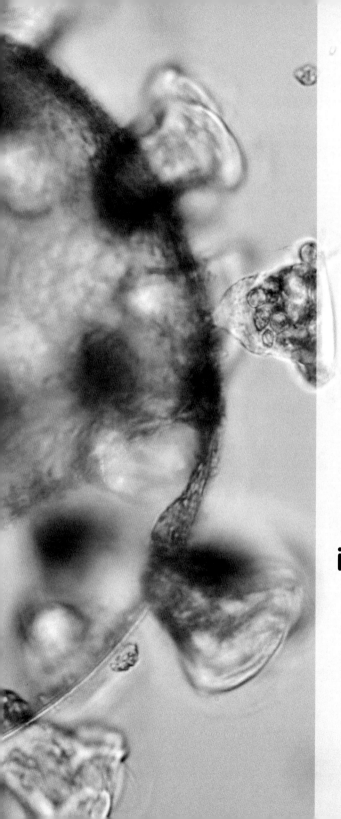

These invaders are composed only of one cell. These germs love to be in moist places. Often, protozoa spread diseases through contaminated water. Intestinal infections are caused by protozoa. This includes diarrhoea.

Why do Germs Make us Sick?

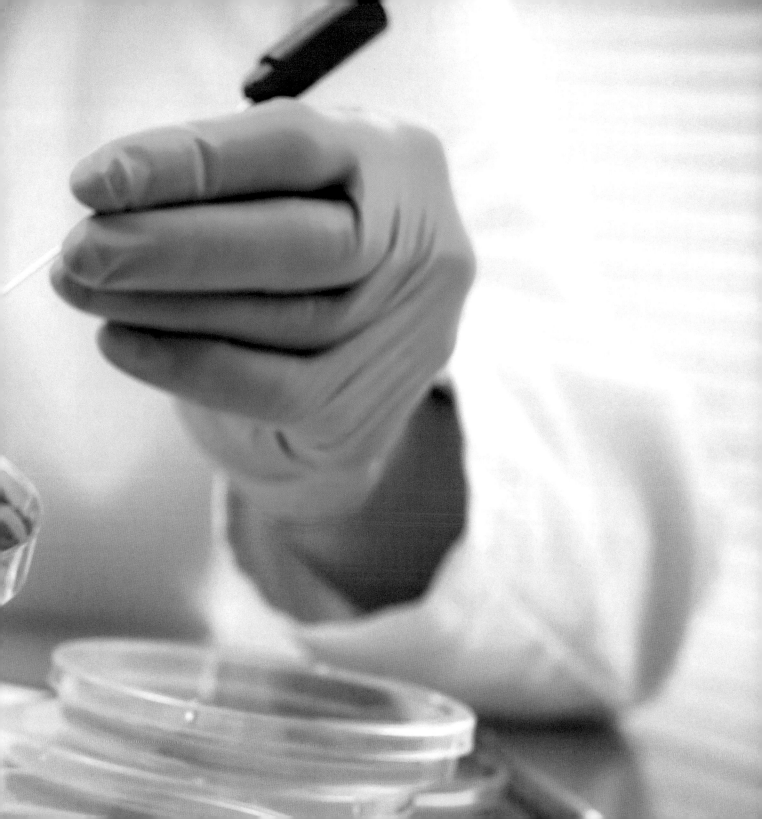

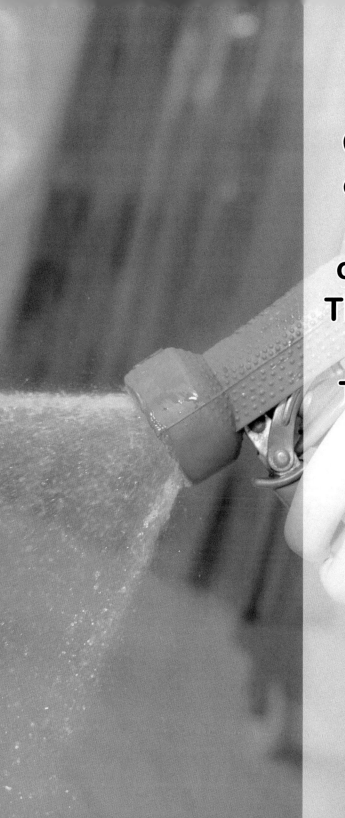

Once germs get into our bodies, they use our nutrients and consume our energy. They work hard to stay long in our bodies. They produce toxins. These are poison-like proteins which cause common infections. Toxins cause symptoms such as diarrhoea, fever and cough.

Doctors will be able to identify what kinds of germs live inside our body by taking samples of our urine, blood, and stool. By doing laboratory tests, the doctor will know which tiny invaders in our body are trying to make us sick.

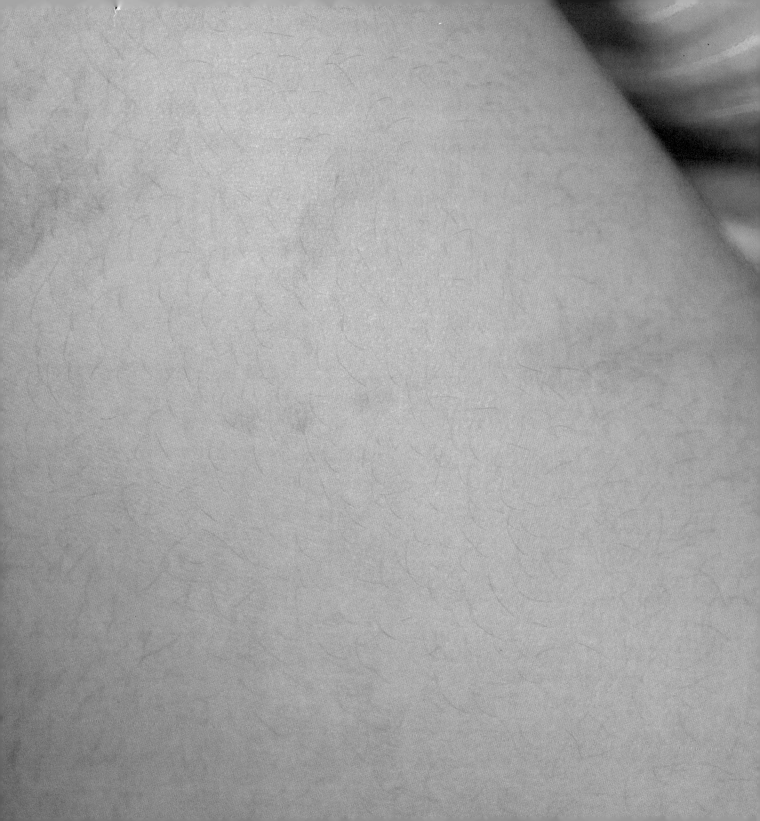

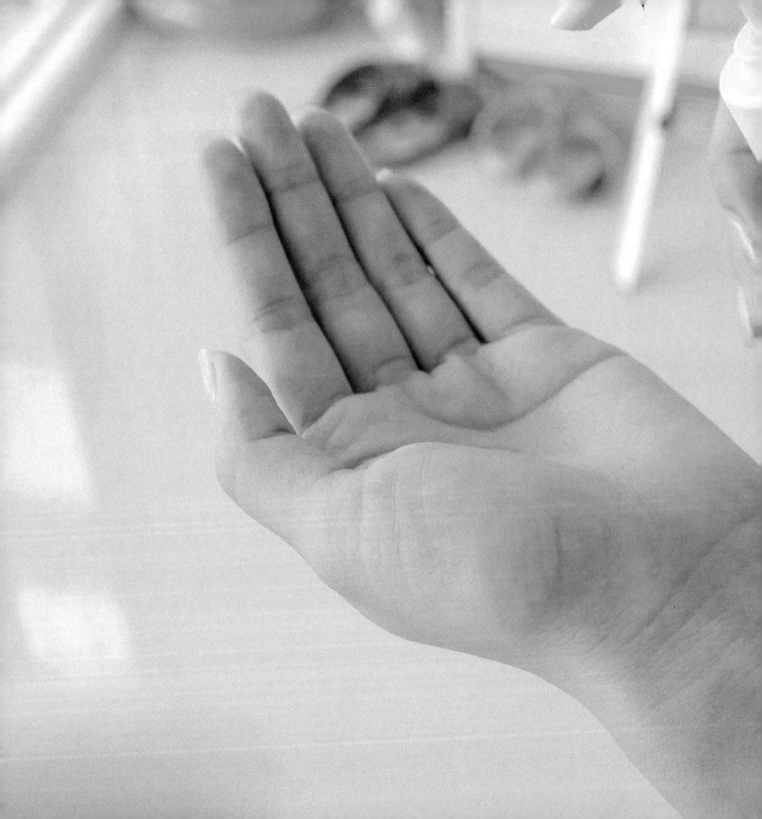

How to Get Rid of These Germs

Germs spread easily. They can easily spread through air and water. Simple shaking hands and touching contaminated objects will let these germs get into our body. One of the most effective ways of protecting ourselves from acquiring these germs is by hand washing. We should wash our hands regularly. Scare out germs by using soap and water. Beat these tiny invaders. Do it now. They have no right to stay in our body.

Visit

BABY PROFESSOR
EDUCATION KIDS

www.BabyProfessorBooks.com

to download Free Baby Professor eBooks
and view our catalog of new and exciting
Children's Books

Made in the USA
Las Vegas, NV
05 February 2024

85294373R00026